Billy the Bookworm stated quite loudly, in this book here..
Of Butterflies, and Bella, it is so very clear!
That they are special by far, above all other creatures.
They have very wonderful and unique features!
They live different lives than we!
What an amazing story there is to see.
Because they live four different ways.
And they can live for many days..
Either a month or up to nine, or more!
They're special indeed, we can't ignore!
Depending on where they are born.
And if the Milkweed is near the corn!
In this book they mention poison and pesticides!!
It says that the butterflies are fading...and besides.
It's not good for the rest of us too.
This sounds bad, what should we do?

Butterflies are very lucky indeed!
They get to visit all the flowers and feed!
Baby caterpillars only eat Milkweed.
When they're young, it's all they need.
They eat and eat and shed their skin.
Now it's just where they once have been!
But underneath is a brand new one.
So eat and eat and eat for fun!
It's what they do when they come out.
Then...they change for a wonderful new route!

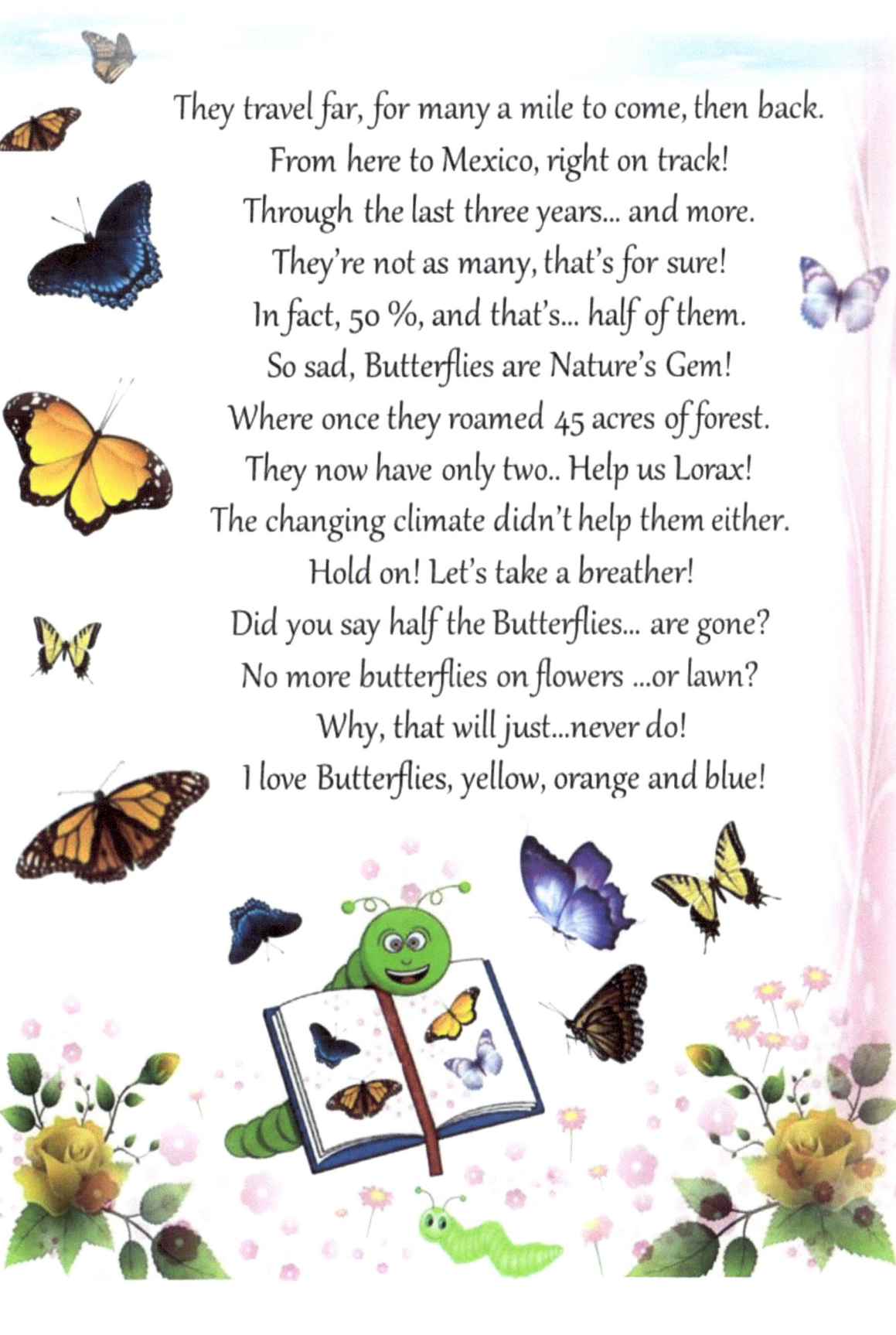

They travel far, for many a mile to come, then back.
From here to Mexico, right on track!
Through the last three years... and more.
They're not as many, that's for sure!
In fact, 50 %, and that's... half of them.
So sad, Butterflies are Nature's Gem!
Where once they roamed 45 acres of forest.
They now have only two.. Help us Lorax!
The changing climate didn't help them either.
Hold on! Let's take a breather!
Did you say half the Butterflies... are gone?
No more butterflies on flowers ...or lawn?
Why, that will just...never do!
I love Butterflies, yellow, orange and blue!

Like little Olympic travelers... they carry the torch.
To the Mountains... over valley and gorge!
Mother Nature's compass shows them the way.
A Billion will begin their 2,500 mile journey today!
Through the ages they have winged their way to Mexico.
Seeking their home for the Winter, Mother Nature knows!
The Sierra Mountains are their home far away.
Perfect temperature... Coming from Canada way!
They pass the torch to their next of kin.
And this is the way....it's always been!
Their next generation arrives just in time.
Completing their mission, and this page's rhyme!:)

Come one, Come All! Heed our call!
We need your help, your energy...your Spirit!
Listen now....listen well... Can you hear it?
It's the sound of one voice in the darkness..
Crying out for help....Are we there?
Do we listen...do we dare?
Dare to help.. To make ...a difference?
Yes...for now our efforts... will bring...significance!
I say here and now, let's get it together!
Let's make a pact to change it..**Forever!**

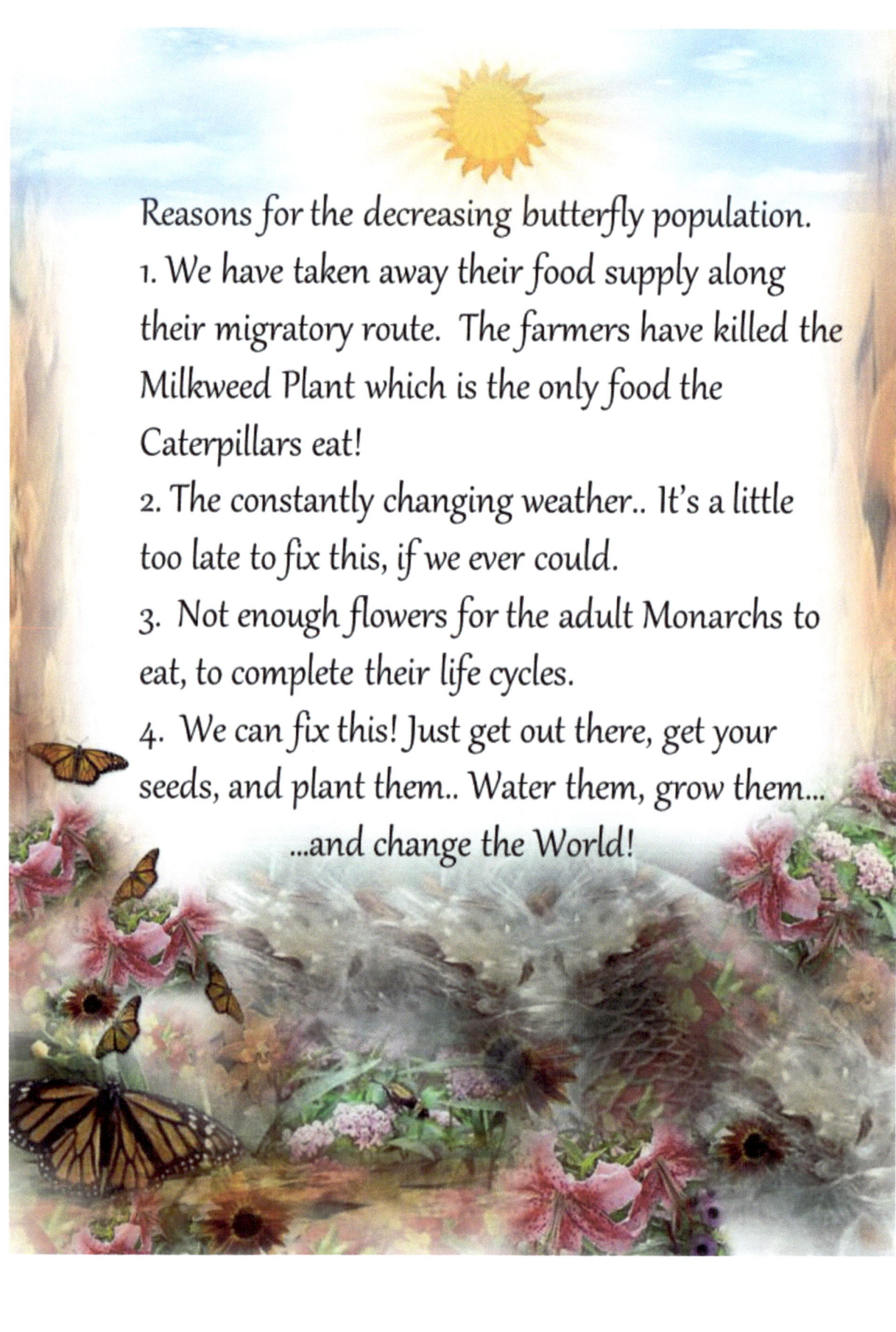

Reasons for the decreasing butterfly population.

1. We have taken away their food supply along their migratory route. The farmers have killed the Milkweed Plant which is the only food the Caterpillars eat!

2. The constantly changing weather.. It's a little too late to fix this, if we ever could.

3. Not enough flowers for the adult Monarchs to eat, to complete their life cycles.

4. We can fix this! Just get out there, get your seeds, and plant them.. Water them, grow them...
...and change the World!

Here's the map of the 2014 Migratory Patterns of
The Monarch Butterfly.. Compliments of Journey North.
Monarch **Butterfly Migration** |
Journey North Citizen Science ...
www.learner.org/jnorth/**monarch**/

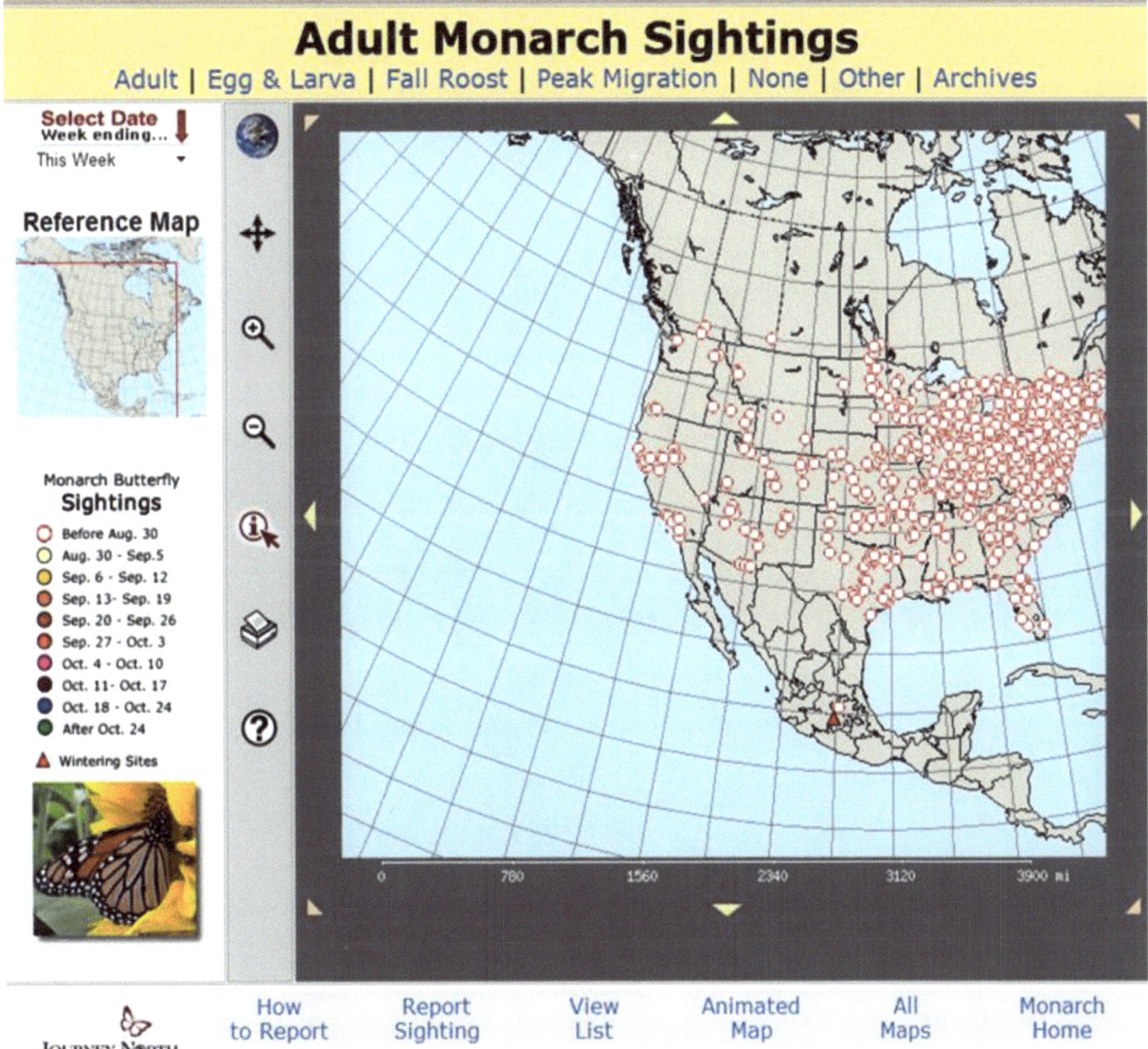

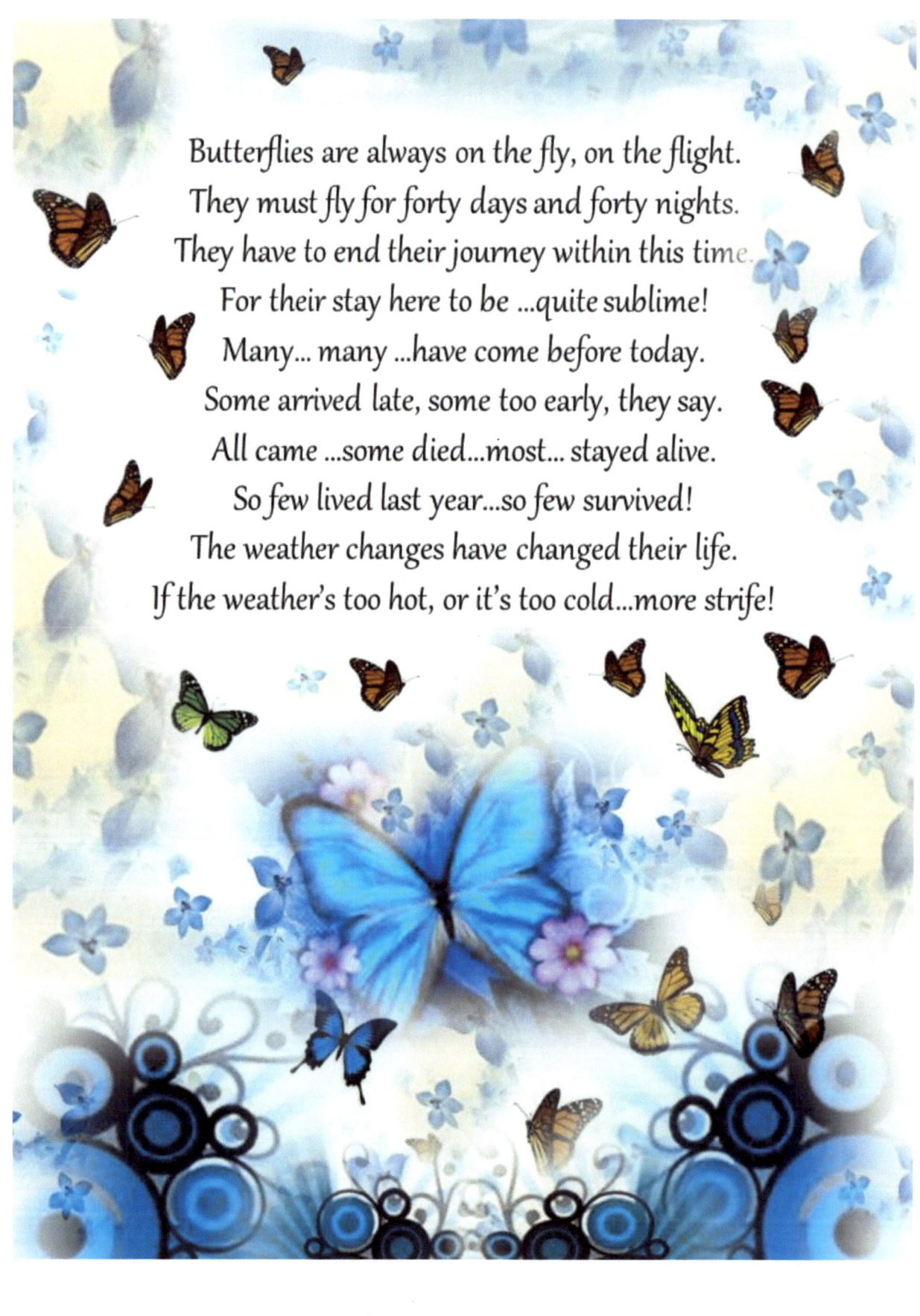

Butterflies are always on the fly, on the flight.
They must fly for forty days and forty nights.
They have to end their journey within this time.
For their stay here to be ...quite sublime!
Many... many ...have come before today.
Some arrived late, some too early, they say.
All came ...some died...most... stayed alive.
So few lived last year...so few survived!
The weather changes have changed their life.
If the weather's too hot, or it's too cold...more strife!

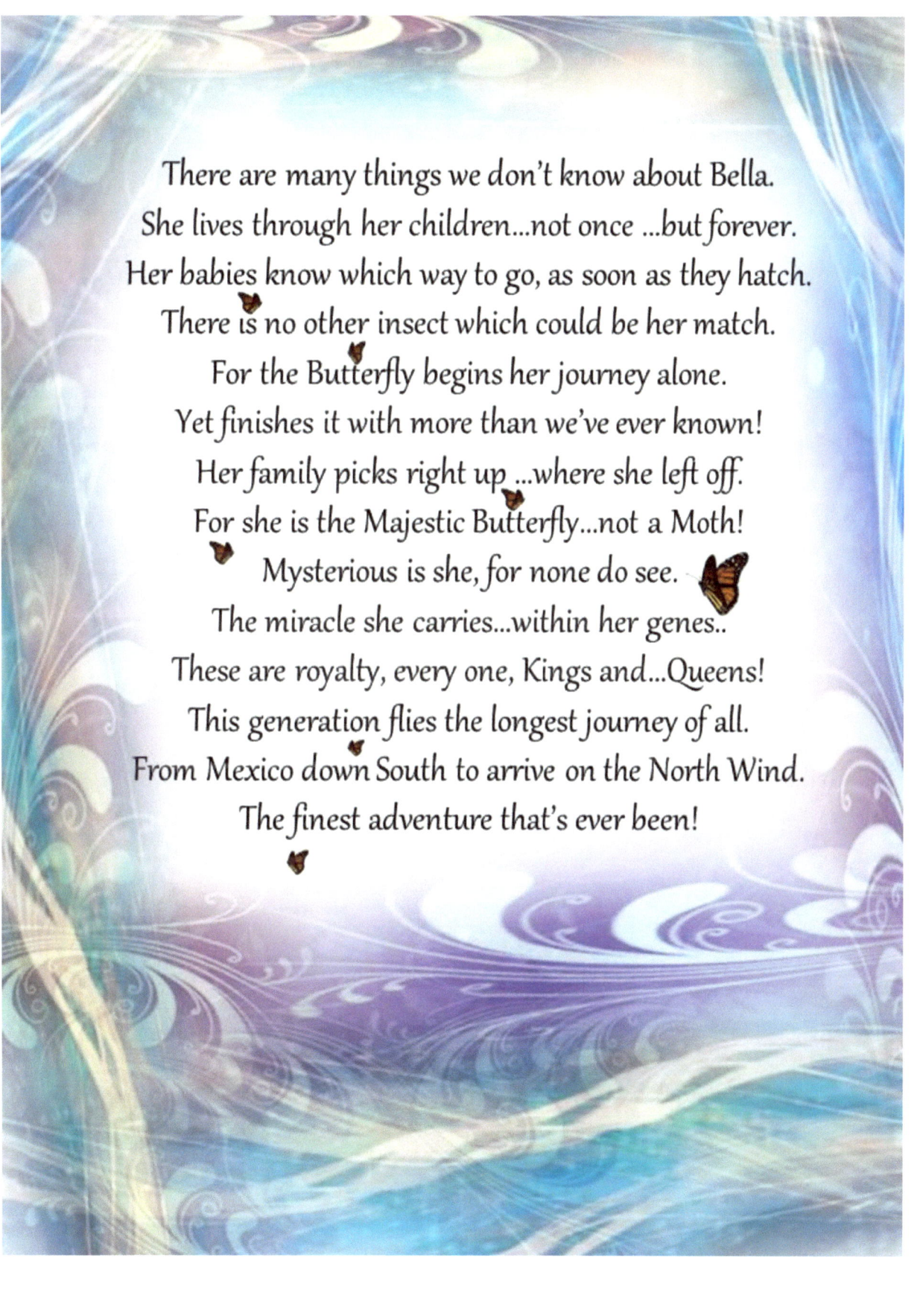

There are many things we don't know about Bella.
She lives through her children...not once ...but forever.
Her babies know which way to go, as soon as they hatch.
There is no other insect which could be her match.
For the Butterfly begins her journey alone.
Yet finishes it with more than we've ever known!
Her family picks right up ...where she left off.
For she is the Majestic Butterfly...not a Moth!
Mysterious is she, for none do see.
The miracle she carries...within her genes..
These are royalty, every one, Kings and...Queens!
This generation flies the longest journey of all.
From Mexico down South to arrive on the North Wind.
The finest adventure that's ever been!

The last generation...is the over-wintering generation.

They vacation in Mexico until they seek their new location.

In the early spring, they fly north to the southern United States.

Here they will find their perfect lifetime mates.

Then they will find the most perfect spot.

To lay their eggs...not too damp.. Not too hot!

These are the royalty of Monarch Butterflies!

These lucky ones live 8 months or more!

They tell the final story of Bella and the four..

An amazing story of Mother Nature and her Magical ways!

The kind that does.....most certainly... Amaze!

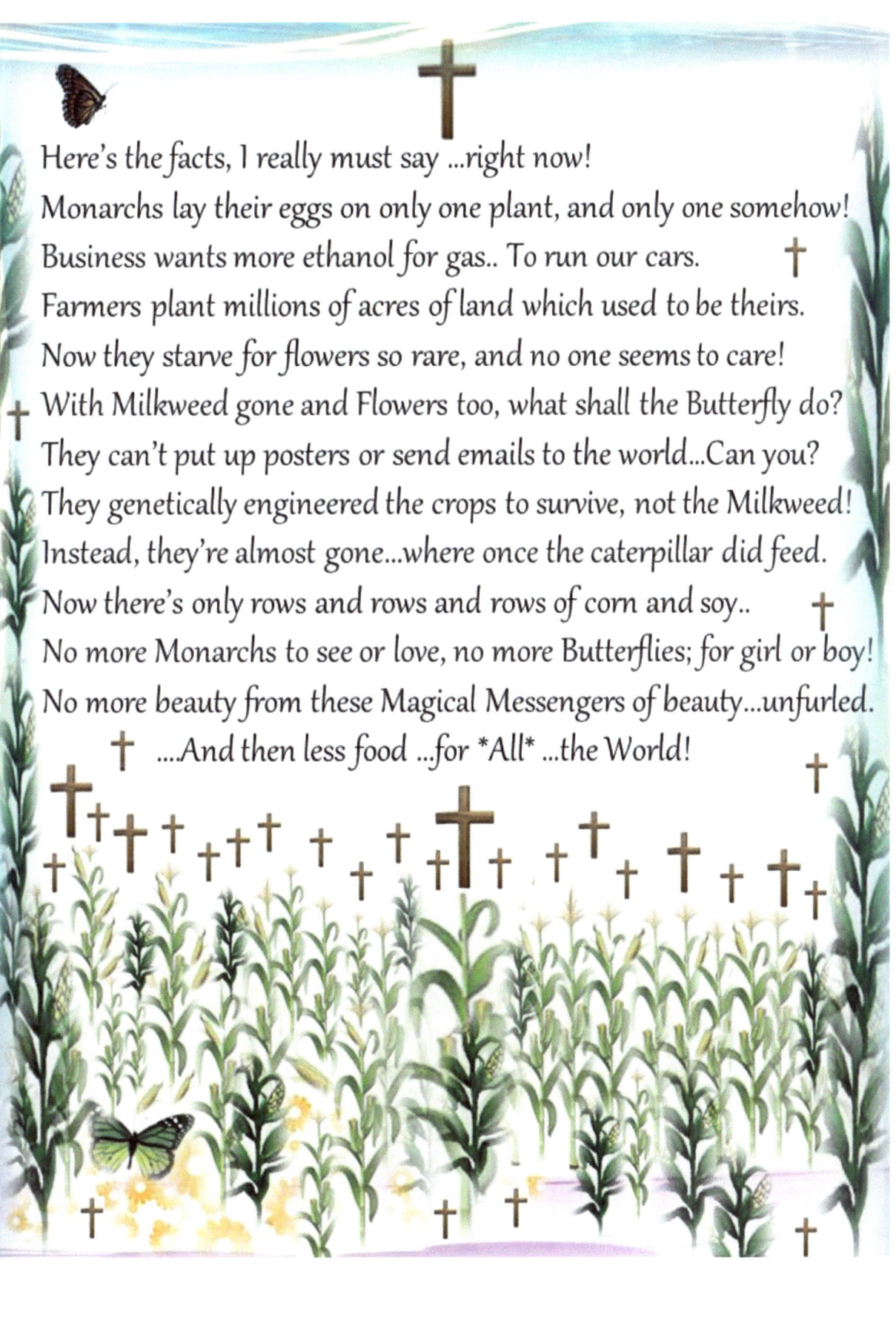

Here's the facts, I really must say ...right now!

Monarchs lay their eggs on only one plant, and only one somehow!

Business wants more ethanol for gas.. To run our cars.

Farmers plant millions of acres of land which used to be theirs.

Now they starve for flowers so rare, and no one seems to care!

With Milkweed gone and Flowers too, what shall the Butterfly do?

They can't put up posters or send emails to the world...Can you?

They genetically engineered the crops to survive, not the Milkweed!

Instead, they're almost gone...where once the caterpillar did feed.

Now there's only rows and rows and rows of corn and soy..

No more Monarchs to see or love, no more Butterflies; for girl or boy!

No more beauty from these Magical Messengers of beauty...unfurled.

....And then less food ...for *All* ...the World!

It says here, that they know just where they're going, every day!
Something inside of them... just shows them their way.
Must be Mother Nature, she's like that, you know.
She whispers to all living things... the right way to go!
Bella has a very busy schedule, it seems.
In February and March, the life cycles begin their schemes.
They come out of hibernation, looking for a friend.
They search for signals that the male often sends.
Through March and April they plan the way.
To lay their eggs, soon...this very day!
The new Mothers hide their eggs in a very safe place.
Each on Milkweed plants so as to not.. leave a trace.
Babies safe and hatching soon, they travel across the moon.
In four days the babies hatch, so soon?
To live out their lives away from them..
Perhaps upon a milkweed stem!

Don't be afraid, you little one..
Soon you'll join me for some fun!
I know it's hard to know right now.
But you will fly away somehow..
With wings so strong and colors bright,
You'll travel the day into the night.
Listen now. For I know for sure.
Your life is changing...from immature...
To full-fledged beauty with wings to fly.
To fly so high..up ...up ...Up... into the sky!

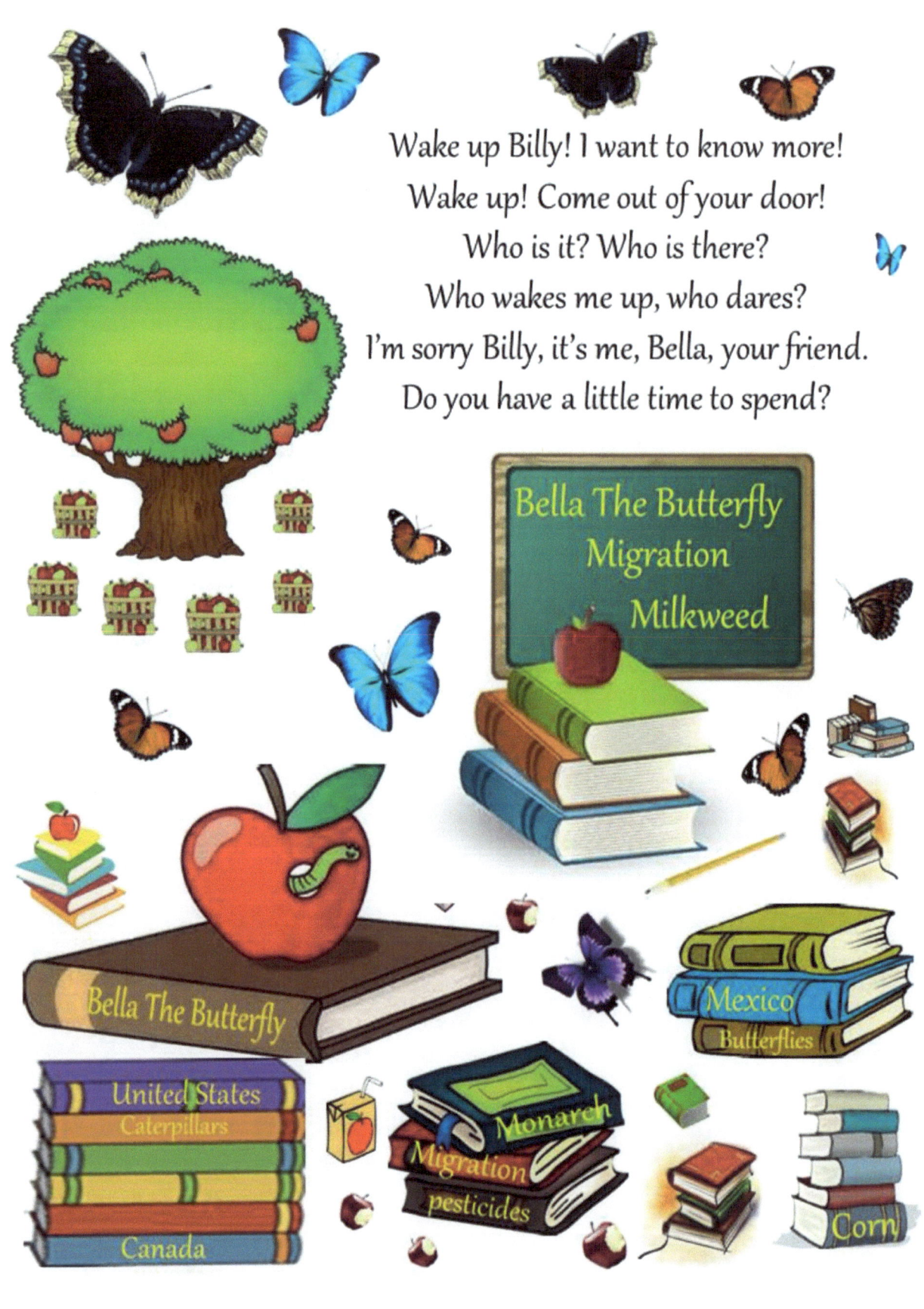

Wake up Billy! I want to know more!
Wake up! Come out of your door!
Who is it? Who is there?
Who wakes me up, who dares?
I'm sorry Billy, it's me, Bella, your friend.
Do you have a little time to spend?

Milkweed + Caterpillar = Butterfly
No Milkweed = No Butterflies
No Butterflies = No Pollination

of Flowers Vegetables
No Flowers = No Seeds
No seeds = No Food!
No Food = No Life

Get it Now?

Today's Lessons

We have to save our Beautiful Butterflies!
Then we save the Bumble bees and Fireflies.
One by one, we fix what we've destroyed.
We make those contracts, null and void.
For if we don't and we allow this to happen..
Old Mother Nature, sad and angry, will come a tappin'!
Change the course or blow out to Sea.
Know the way or they'll be lost forever, never free!
Free to live their lives, or free to fly the skies.
So....I propose... we get together and save them all!
We save the red, blue, and yellow..large and small.

Instructions For Planting Milkweed and Butterfly Flowers

1. Read the Instructions on the Seed Package
2. Do everything it says to do....
3. Always wear gloves when planting.
4. Make sure your new plants get watered.
5. Plant your seeds in a very Sunny spot.
6. Sometimes, the soil needs fertilizer.
7. Now, sit back and watch your babies grow!

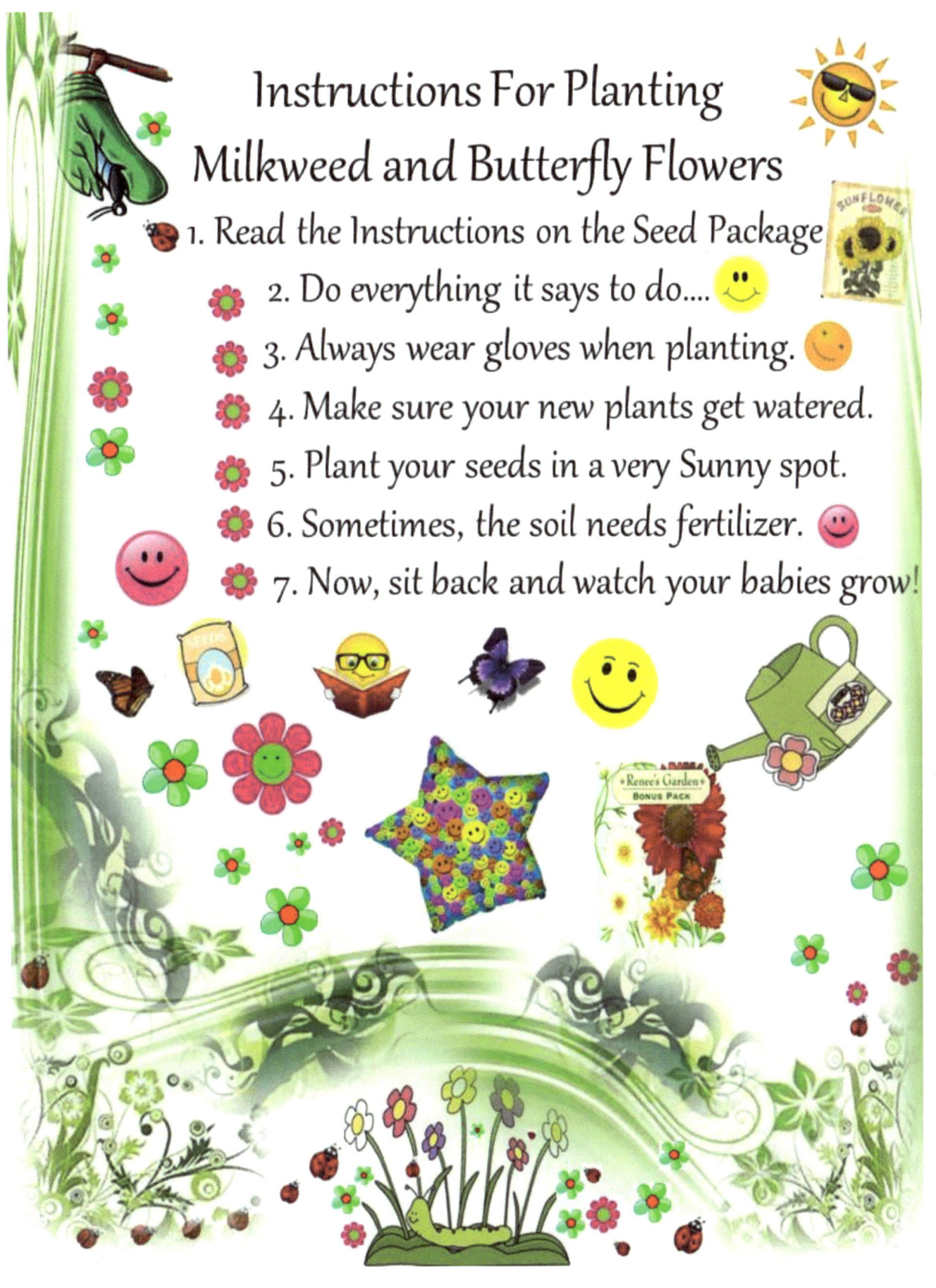

The Miracle begins here.. in this place.
When all of the butterflies arrive with grace.
They flutter and fly in secret syncopation.
Where all of them come for... reintegration!
As all secrets in Nature, only they know.
This is for them, this is their show!
This solemn ceremony shared only by them.
Nature's bounty, Mother Nature's...Gem!

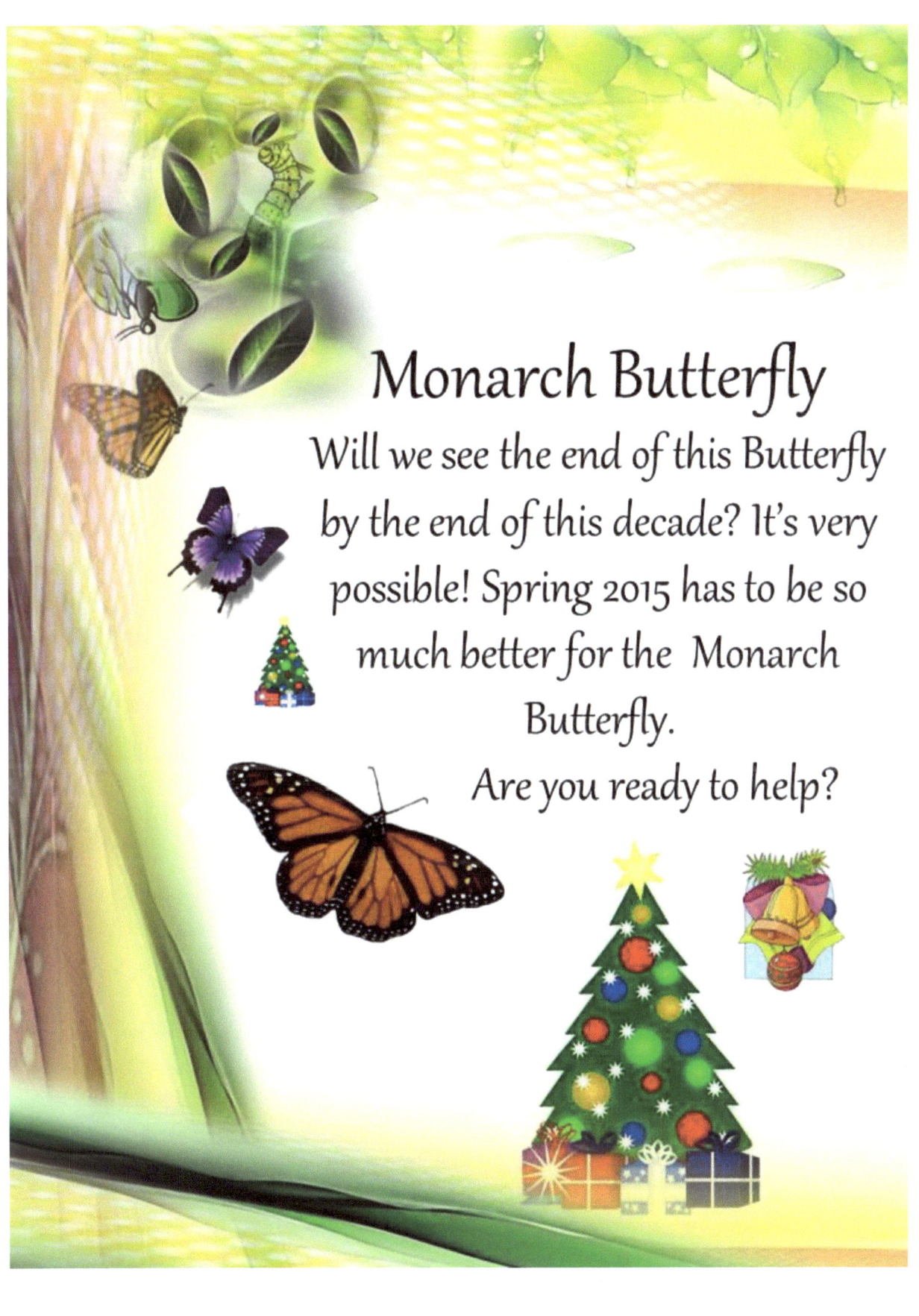

Monarch Butterfly

Will we see the end of this Butterfly by the end of this decade? It's very possible! Spring 2015 has to be so much better for the Monarch Butterfly.

Are you ready to help?

This very Winter 2014-2015, I would like for all of us to say..
I pledge to help the Monarch Butterfly...today!

_____ Name

_____ State

_____ Date

All we need is...Love!

From one lover of Butterflies to another,
let me just say...
Sometimes we have to think more of others ...
...in a kindlier way.
This is your opportunity to make a big difference..
Indeed....to be someone of...Great Significance!

To : The World
Please Help!
Plant Milkweed Seeds!
Respond A.S.A.P.

VOL. 150, NO. 2　　　AUGUST 1976

NATIONAL GEOGRAPHIC

OFFICIAL JOURNAL OF THE NATIONAL GEOGRAPHIC SOCIETY WASHINGTON, D.C.

Ode to The Butterfly

Butterfly, Butterfly, flying so high!
If I could sprout wings..why..
I would.. in a heart beat ...of a gentle Fairy...
I would fly so fast and never tarry!
Oh to be such a beautiful sight.
And be remembered by my wondrous flight..
To soar high above the rest.
And fly on the Winds... like the best!
Would be my wish if God did grant...
Just to fly and fly ...across Sea and sand!

Monarch Butterfly Seeds

Monarchs love bright orange flowers. Indeed they are attracted to them and some Milkweed Plants have bright orange flowers. Some have yellow and pink flowers. Monarch Caterpillars go from Milkweed to the nectar of Flowers in their Butterfly form. They need Flowers to gain strength for their long Migratory journey to The Sierra Mountains. If they can't find flowers or Milkweed plants they are doomed, and will not make it. We need to help them!

R.S.V.P. 2015

You're invited to attend The World's

1st Annual Meeting of...

Save The Butterflies!

Bella The Butterfly
by Adrienne

Bella The Butterfly

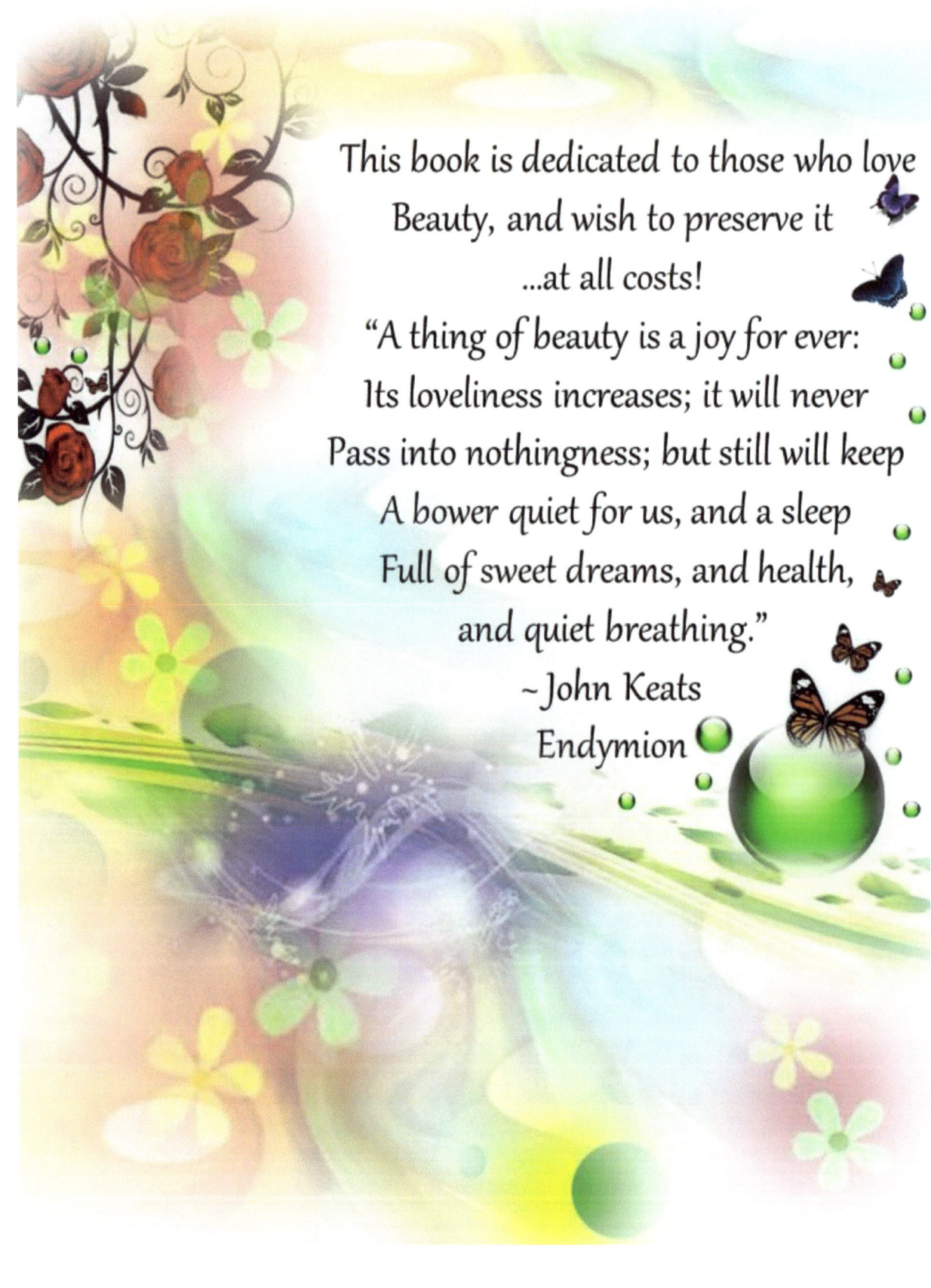

This book is dedicated to those who love
Beauty, and wish to preserve it
...at all costs!
"A thing of beauty is a joy for ever:
Its loveliness increases; it will never
Pass into nothingness; but still will keep
A bower quiet for us, and a sleep
Full of sweet dreams, and health,
and quiet breathing."
~John Keats
Endymion

Instructions For Planting
Milkweed and Butterfly Flowers
1. Read the Instructions on the Seed Package.
2. Do everything it says to do....
3. Always wear gloves when planting.
4. Make sure your new plants get watered.
5. Plant your seeds in a very Sunny spot.
6. Sometimes, the soil needs fertilizer.
7. Now, sit back and watch your babies grow!

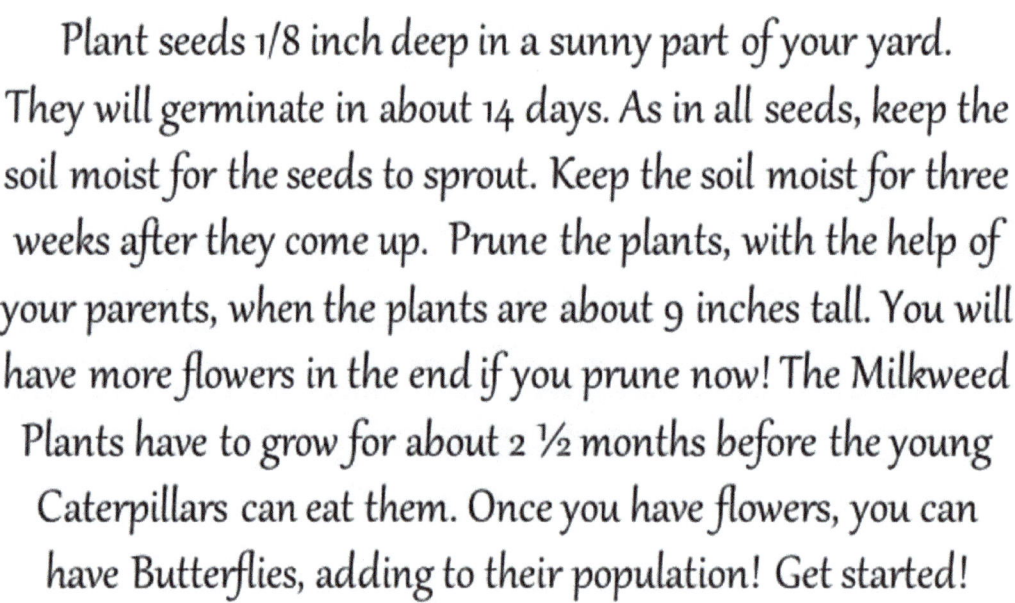

Plant seeds 1/8 inch deep in a sunny part of your yard. They will germinate in about 14 days. As in all seeds, keep the soil moist for the seeds to sprout. Keep the soil moist for three weeks after they come up. Prune the plants, with the help of your parents, when the plants are about 9 inches tall. You will have more flowers in the end if you prune now! The Milkweed Plants have to grow for about 2 ½ months before the young Caterpillars can eat them. Once you have flowers, you can have Butterflies, adding to their population! Get started!

Please visit ....
Live Monarch, a website devoted to saving the
Monarch Butterfly.. at
Live Monarch Foundation One seed can
change the World.
www.**livemonarch**.com

One Seed At A Time!

This very Winter 2014-2015, I would like for all of us to say..
I pledge to help the Monarch Butterfly...today!

_____ Name

_____ State

_____ Date

Pass it Along!

This very Winter 2014-2015, I would like for all of us to say..
I pledge to help the Monarch Butterfly...today!

_____ Name

_____ State

_____ Date

Pass it Along!

This very Winter 2014-2015, I would like for all of us to say..
I pledge to help the Monarch Butterfly...today!

_____ Name

_____ State

_____ Date

Pass it Along!

This very Winter 2014-2015, I would like for all of us to say..
I pledge to help the Monarch Butterfly...today!

_____ Name

_____ State

_____ Date

Pass it Along!

I have always thought the Monarch Butterfly one of those
magical wondrous gifts of Nature. One which has always
been a part of my life. Who does not love Butterflies? What's
not to love? Their graceful flight of fancy, as they gather
sweet nectar from the beautiful flowers. A thing of beauty is
a joy forever. It's beauty does not fade or diminish as it
continues it's mystical ancient journey from one land to
another. It spreads joyful imaginations where ever it goes!
We can save it! Please do!

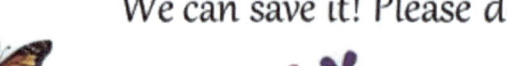